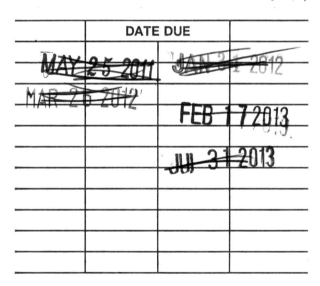

The Urbana Free Library

To renew materials call
217-367-4057

Even or Odd?

Joanne Mattern

www.rourkepublishing.com

www.rourkepublishing.com

PHOTO CREDITS: Cover: © fredfroese; Title Page: © Newlight; Page 3: © Christopher Hall; Page 5: © Robyn Mackenzie; Page 7: © James Trice; Page 8, 9, 11: © joingate; Page 12, 15: © DNY59; Page 13: © Ewa Brozek; Page 16, 17, 19: © Michelle Minix; Page 20, 23: © Craig Veltri; Page 21: © Keith Bell

Edited by Luana Mitten

Cover and Interior design by Tara Raymo

Library of Congress Cataloging-in-Publication Data

Mattern, Joanne, 1963-
 Even or odd? / Joanne Mattern.
    p. cm. -- (Little world math concepts)
 Includes bibliographical references and index.
 ISBN 978-1-61590-292-7 (Hard Cover) (alk. paper)
 ISBN 978-1-61590-531-7 (Soft Cover)
 1. Number concept--Juvenile literature. I. Title.
 QA141.15.M278 2011
 513.2--dc22
                                    2010009893

Rourke Publishing
Printed in the United States of America, North Mankato, Minnesota
010311
123010LP-A

www.rourkepublishing.com - rourke@rourkepublishing.com
Post Office Box 643328 Vero Beach, Florida 32964

Some numbers are even.
Some numbers are odd. What is
the difference?

Even numbers can be grouped by twos.

Even

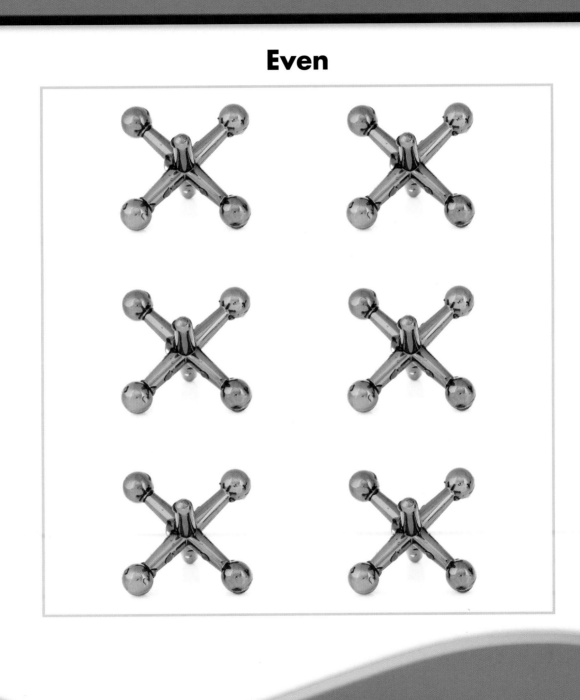

Odd numbers cannot be grouped by twos.

Odd

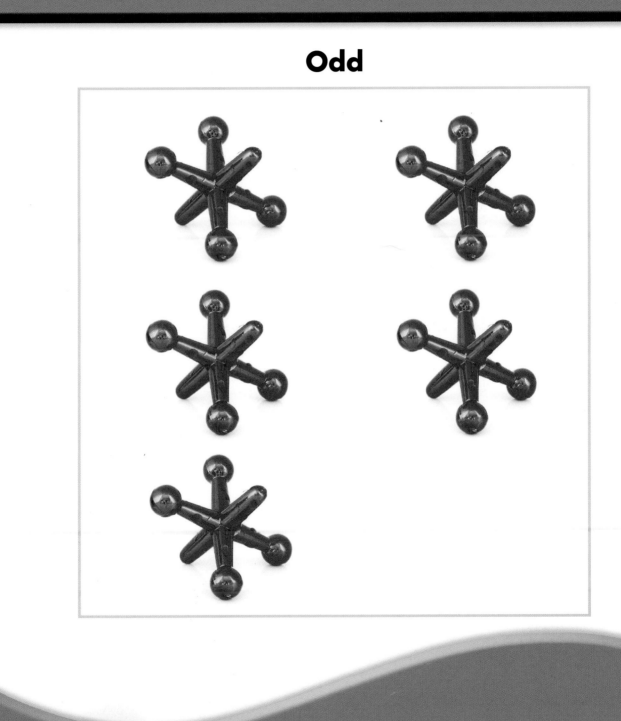

Which group of cars has an
even number?

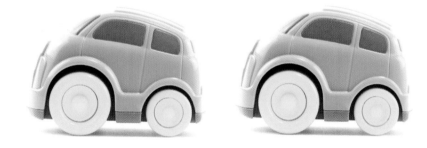

There is an even number of red cars! The red cars can be grouped by twos.

Even

Which group of fruit has an even number?

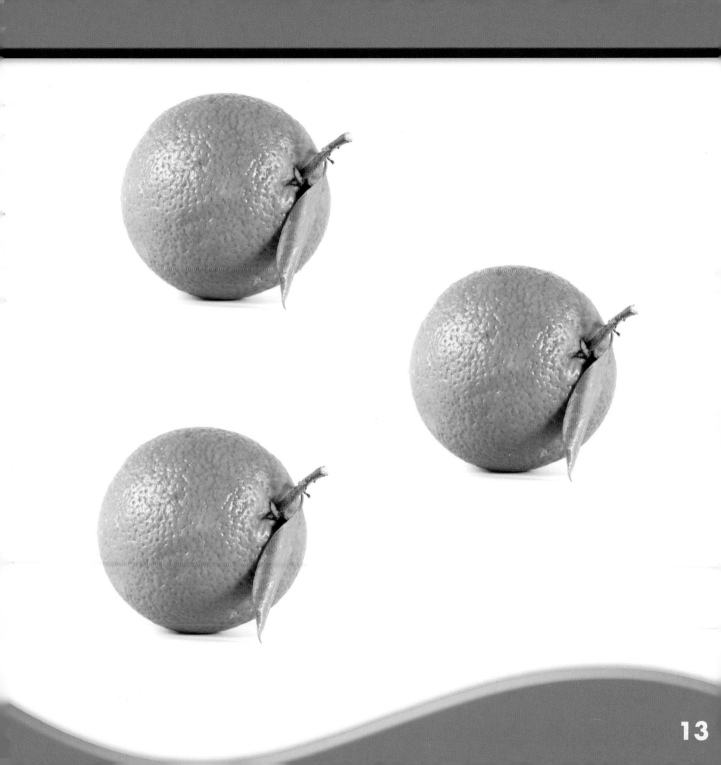

There is an even number of apples.
The apples can be grouped by twos.

Even

Which group of shapes has an odd number?

There is an odd number of squares. The squares cannot be grouped by twos.

Odd

Which group of balls has an odd number?

There is an odd number of purple balls. The purple balls cannot be grouped by twos.

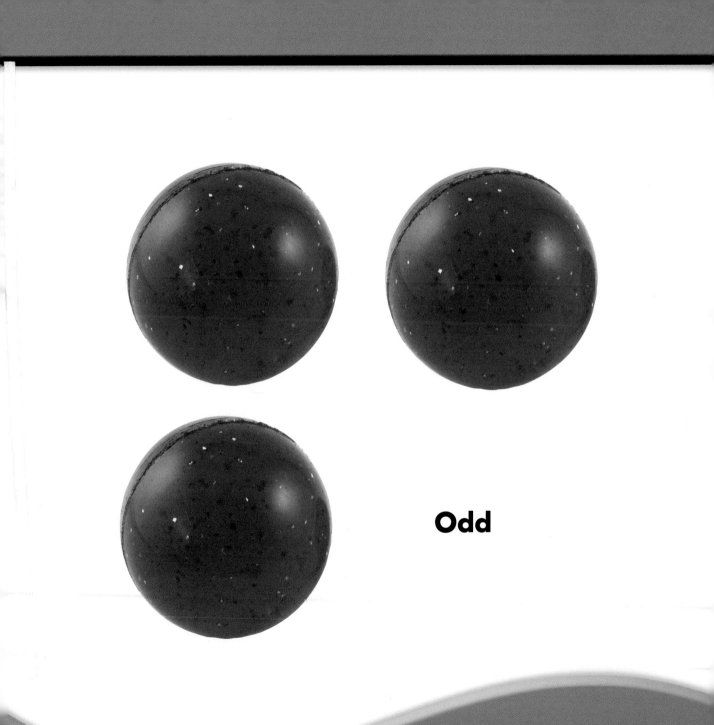

Odd

Index

Websites

www.aaamath.com/g25a2-evenodd.html

www.supereacherworksheets.com/odd-even.html

www.softschools.com/math/games/odd_even_number_games.jsp

About the Author

Joanne Mattern has an even number of children (4) and an odd number of pets (7). She is not sure if she has written an even or an odd number of books because she has written so many. She lives with her family in New York State, in a town that has an odd number of letters in it.